CONQUERING DIET DRUG ABUSE

CONQUERING DIET DRUG ABUSE

NICHOLAS FAULKNER AND KARA WILLIAMS

ROSEN
PUBLISHING™

New York

Published in 2016 by The Rosen Publishing Group, Inc.
29 East 21st Street, New York, NY 10010

First Edition

Library of Congress Cataloging-in-Publication Data

Faulkner, Nicholas.
 Conquering diet drug abuse / Nicholas Faulkner and Kara Williams. – First
edition.
     pages cm. – (Conquering eating disorders)
 Audience: Grades 7-12.
 Includes index.
 ISBN 978-1-4994-6197-8 (library bound)
 1. Appetite depressants–Health aspects–Juvenile literature. 2. Weight loss
preparations–Health aspects–Juvenile literature. 3. Medication abuse–Juvenile literature. I. Williams, Kara. II. Title.
 RM332.3.F38 2016
 615.7'8–dc23
                                2015012869

For many of the images in this book, the people photographed are models.
The depictions do not imply actual situations or events.

Manufactured in the United States of America

CONTENTS

The World of Diet Drugs

People have been trying to lose weight throughout history, so diet drugs are not new. What also isn't new is the danger that they can pose. There's no such thing as quick weight loss, which many diet drugs promise. In helping you try to lose weight quickly, diet drugs can threaten your health and even cause you to put on more pounds. Americans live in a society that is obsessed with weight, body shape, fitness, and dieting. According to a 2013 *U.S. News & World Report* article, Americans spend more than $60 billion annually to try to lose weight.

The American culture often sends out messages that you have to be thin to be desirable and successful. These messages can be seen everywhere—on television, in magazines and advertisements, and in the movies. The media encourage people to believe that they must be thin to be accepted by others. In response to these messages, many people go on diets to try to achieve a physical body shape that is often impossible for the average American to reach.

Everyone Wants to Lose Weight

Millions of people in the United States are trying to lose weight every day. The weight-loss business is booming. A wide variety

As long as there are people who want to lose weight, there will be fad diet drugs. Often, these products make false promises and can be harmful to your health.

of products are on the market today that promise to help people shed their unwanted pounds.

Some products can be bought by anyone in local drugstores or health-food stores. Some drugs claim to be natural and safe aids to losing weight. Others are new and untested. There are also products that require a doctor's prescription. Many are marketed with misleading or false claims about their powers and side effects. Some people also use products that are not meant for weight-loss purposes because they believe those products will help them lose weight.

What most people don't realize is that many of these products do not help anyone lose weight permanently. In fact, they can have dangerous, and even deadly, side effects. Knowing the facts about the dangers of diet drugs will help you understand the importance of leading a healthy lifestyle—without diets or diet drugs. Developing your self-esteem and a positive body image are your best tools in preventing an eating disorder.

History has proven that there is only one tried-and-true way to lose weight, and that's by not dieting. Maintaining healthy eating habits, exercising regularly, setting realistic weight goals, and developing a positive body image are the only proven ways to lose the pounds and keep them off.

Diet Drugs and Easy Access

There are countless brands of diet drugs on the market today, and more and more are being sold over-the-counter, meaning that they do not require a doctor's prescription to purchase. Over-the-counter diet drugs are often sold in drugstores and health-food stores, as well as in supermarkets. No restrictions are placed on

Over-the-counter diet drugs are often sold in drugstores and health-food stores, as well as in supermarkets.

the sale of these drugs. Anyone can buy as many products as often as he or she wants. However, this does not mean over-the-counter diet drugs have never presented any health problems.

For several decades, the main ingredient in most over-the-counter diet drugs (including Accutrim and Dexatrim) was called phenylpropanolamine, or PPA. PPA is a stimulant that resembles the illegal drugs known as amphetamines (speed). PPA can cause high blood pressure, anxiety, and nervousness. In addition to side effects, there is no proof that PPA helps people lose weight permanently. In fact, PPA has been banned in many countries. The US Bureau of Consumer Protection removed these dangerous weight-loss products from the market. Unfortunately, many other unsafe diet products continue to be sold.

A Yale University School of Medicine study found that women who took over-the-counter diet pills with PPA were up to fifteen times more likely to suffer a stroke. In response, the Food and Drug Administration (FDA) advised consumers to stop taking PPA (also found in nasal decongestants) and asked the makers of those drugs to take them off the market.

Although most drug companies complied by taking PPA products off the shelves, they also found ways to work around the FDA advisory by reformulating products and renaming them. Ineffective products still find their way into the marketplace.

An Abundance of False Advertising

Some people who want to lose weight turn to diet pills because they believe the pills will help them become thinner. Many diet drug companies make false promises about the effectiveness of products.

These products seem to provide easy and fast solutions to losing weight without exercising. In commercials, ads, and e-mailed spam, the companies show before and after pictures of "real"

Claiming that a product provides a benefit when it really doesn't is known as false advertising. Many diet drug companies are guilty of this practice, and the government is cracking down on them.

people who have used their products. This sends the message that if you use their products, you, too, will become a slimmer and more attractive person in no time at all.

Sometimes it can be very hard not to believe these claims, and many people buy into the advertisements. It seems to be so easy to go to the drugstore around the corner, pick up a box of diet drugs, and immediately start losing weight. But there are no such easy answers. If you read the fine print in the advertisements for these products, you will discover that the drugs will not help you lose weight permanently.

Before you think about using an over-the-counter diet drug, it's important that you investigate the risks, as well as consider the reasons why you think you need to lose weight.

Read the Labels

All manufacturers of diet drugs are required by the FDA to have a label that lists the following:

• The active ingredients in the drug
• Any other ingredients
• The drug's intended purpose or purposes
• Directions for use, including recommended dosages
• Known side effects
• Groups put at risk by the drug

Diet drugs and other over-the-counter drugs cannot be sold without such a label. The label is supposed to protect the consumer, but it also protects the company manufacturing the drug. If the consumer does not follow the directions, the drug company can deny any responsibility for harmful reactions.

Labels on diet drugs are sometimes hard to understand. Although all the information required by the FDA is on the back of the box, it is often printed in very small letters. The information may also be hard to detect because slogans and claims are often printed on the packages in big, bold letters that draw your attention away from other information. These are designed to boost sales of the product. They make the diet drug seem safe and effective. The slogans on diet drugs are easy to read. It takes time and effort to read the information required by the FDA. Yet it's also important to know that many diet drug manufacturers try to work around FDA regulations, and others just ignore them. The FDA is not always able to pursue all consumer complaints.

Don't fall for promises that sound too good to be true. You are putting a drug, a foreign substance, into your body. This drug can have serious effects on your physical health.

Diet Drug Abuse and Why People Do It

Teens who are unhappy with their weight are especially vulnerable to over-the-counter diet drugs. Since the drugs are so easy and cheap to buy, many teens start to abuse them, taking more pills than the recommended dosage. Some think taking more pills will help them lose weight faster.

Because our culture places such importance on thinness, it's easy to fall into the trap of believing that a little pill can make you happier and more attractive. Many people are willing to take serious risks in their efforts to lose weight. In one study conducted by Eating Disorders Awareness and Prevention (EDAP), researchers found that young women are more afraid of becoming fat than they are of losing their parents, getting cancer, or nuclear war. And diet drug companies work hard to target those people who are most worried about their weight.

How Diet Pills Harm Your Body

There are many side effects that occur in young people taking over-the-counter diet pills, including the following:

Taking too much of any drug, including diet drugs, can have dangerous side effects such as dizziness, fainting, or worse.

- Dizziness
- Insomnia
- Confusion
- Headaches
- Anxiety
- Constipation
- Diarrhea
- Trembling hands
- Hypertension
- Rapid heartbeat

If a person is considering an over-the-counter diet pill, he or she should learn all the risk factors of that pill and check with a doctor to make sure that he or she does not have any health problems that may increase the risk of serious side effects.

Ipecac Syrup

Ipecac syrup is sometimes abused by people with bulimia nervosa, an eating disorder in which a person binges on a large amount of food and then purges it by vomiting. Ipecac syrup is a powerful and extremely dangerous substance intended for emergency use only, and today, it's used in very rare circumstances.

For many decades dating back to 1965, it was common for households to have ipecac syrup "on hand" for accidental poisonings. If someone swallowed poison, he or she was given a dose of ipecac syrup. Within a few minutes, he or she would throw up the poison.

In 2003, the American Academy of Pediatrics (AAP) announced that it no longer recommended the use of ipecac syrup and that it should be removed from the home. Vomiting induced by the syrup can put a tremendous amount of strain on the body, and the AAP noted that use of the syrup did not typically help the outcome from accidental poisonings.

Ipecac syrup, however, continues to be sold over the counter. Ingesting ipecac syrup can have the following side effects:

- Become habit forming
- Irritate the blood vessels around the eyes
- Damage the digestive system
- Damage heart tissue
- Increase the risk of cardiac failure (death)

Laxatives

A laxative is a substance that causes bowel movements. Laxatives can be bought over the counter in drugstores and grocery stores. Some teens use a laxative because they believe it will help the food they eat pass right through their bodies. But abusing laxatives can be very dangerous for many reasons. Abusing laxatives dehydrates the body. When the body is dehydrated, it cannot function properly. The body does not have enough water, and it lacks the vital minerals contained in water.

Laxatives can also be addictive. If you use a laxative for more than a week, your body builds up a tolerance and you have to keep increasing the dosage for the laxative to work. Eventually you can become addicted. Cramping, rectal bleeding, stomach pain, and dizziness are only some of the side effects of laxative abuse. It damages the intestines, the liver, and other vital organs.

Diuretics

Diuretics, or water pills, are another product used by some teens and athletes wishing to lose weight. Diuretics contain substances that speed up the action of the kidneys so that a person urinates more frequently. Diuretics can be used to treat various medical conditions, but many dieters use them improperly as weight-loss aids. Some brands of water pills contain ammonium chloride, others

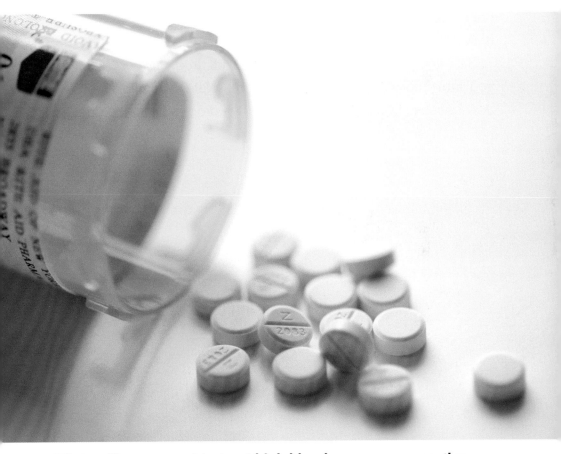

Water pills are meant to treat high blood pressure, congestive heart failure, and other serious medical conditions. They are not meant for dieting.

contain caffeine. Although diuretics reduce liquid in the body, they also decrease the body's potassium and electrolytes, which are needed in regulating bodily functions, including moving nutrients to and wastes from cells.

Water pills reduce the amount of liquid in the body. A short-term loss of a pound or two may result. But the liquid and the weight come back very quickly. The body responds to water pills by holding on to liquid. Water pills upset the normal functions of the body. So-called natural water pills are no better than chemically based diuretics. Both types put you at risk for dehydration and are habit forming.

Diuretics are an example of how diet drugs sometimes trick you into thinking you're losing weight. Water weight is not fat. Just because your scale may say you've dropped pounds doesn't always mean you're losing weight.

MYTHS and *FACTS*

MYTH I'll lose weight faster and keep it off by taking diet drugs.

 Taking diet drugs is not a way to lose weight for the long-term. Diet pills and supplements often lead to rapid weight loss, but you regain your original weight, if not more, just as quickly.

MYTH I only abstain from eating or purge my meals occasionally. I don't necessarily have an eating disorder.

 Eating disorders come in many forms. If you diet in an unhealthy way, you may be heading down the path to having an eating disorder. It's important to catch these behaviors early because the longer they go on, the harder they are to break.

MYTH The diet drugs say they're "natural," so they must be healthy.

 The word "natural" is a marketing term that is often used loosely by companies wanting to sell you their product. The Food and Drug Administration (FDA) does not regulate so-called "natural" weight-loss remedies. Just because it says it's natural doesn't mean it's healthy.

CHAPTER THREE

Requiring a Prescription

One reason why some diet drugs require a prescription is because they can be harmful if not taken appropriately with a doctor's instructions. Sometimes, doctors themselves don't even realize the full dangers. During the 1950s and 1960s, many doctors prescribed amphetamines to patients who wanted to lose weight.

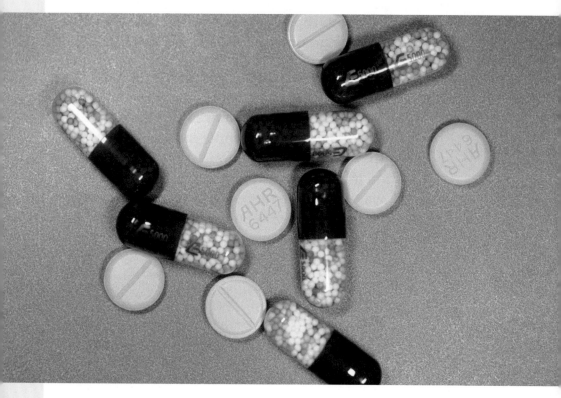

Fen-phen, a combination of fenfluramine and phentermine, is no longer available because it was shown to be potentially fatal.

Amphetamines speed up the body's central nervous system, caus-
ing it to burn more calories. What was not known at the time is that
amphetamines are dangerous and addictive drugs.

People who took amphetamines lost weight, but many also
developed an addiction to the drugs. The drugs increased the body's
heart rate and blood pressure. This caused anxiety, nervousness,
and insomnia. People then used other drugs, called depressants
or downers, to slow down the body's functions. In many cases, the
combination of these two types of drugs proved deadly. When the
federal government and doctors realized the danger that amphetamines posed, restrictions were placed on their use.

Many people believe that any drug prescribed by a physician is
safe and helpful. Unfortunately, this is not always true. Prescription
drugs can also have serious, sometimes deadly, effects on the body.

Diet Crazes of the Past:
Redux and Fen-Phen

In 1996, the Food and Drug Administration (FDA) approved a new
diet drug called dexfenfluramine, marketed under the name Redux.
It was thought by many to be the miracle diet pill. At the same time,
a combination of the drugs fenfluramine and phentermine, or fen-
phen, was being prescribed for weight loss. Although the FDA had
approved fenfluramine many years earlier, it had not approved its
combination with phentermine. Because fenfluramine was found to
make people tired, drug manufacturers mixed it with phentermine,
an amphetamine-like drug, to counteract the drowsiness.

At the time the drugs were made available, scientists knew that
the drugs could cause a fatal heart condition called pulmonary hypertension. But this condition is very rare, and many doctors believed
that the risks of obesity outweighed the risks of the diet pills.

The active ingredients in Redux and fen-phen increase serotonin levels in the brain. Serotonin is a chemical that is basic to a person's emotional and physical sense of well-being. Scientists believe the mood-elevating effect of these drugs helps people to lose weight. Like other drugs, though, Redux and fen-phen also caused side effects. Some of these effects are fatigue, diarrhea, and dry mouth. But over time, the drugs proved even more dangerous.

The Rise of Weight-Loss Centers

The danger of Redux and fen-phen increased partly because the drugs were supposed to be given to people under a doctor's supervision and only for short periods of time—no more than twelve weeks, according to the FDA. But many diet centers, such as Jenny Craig and NutriSystem, began making the drugs available for unlimited periods of time.

Redux and fen-phen were misused by many. People who wanted to lose just a few pounds got prescriptions for Redux and fen-phen from their doctors or weight-loss clinics. But the problem was that many doctors who prescribed the drugs did not discuss their serious side effects with the patients. As a result, many people took the drugs without knowing about the drugs' dangers.

In 1997, Redux and fen-phen were taken off the market by the FDA. Many people had experienced dangerous effects from using these two drugs. Thirty percent of people who were taking the drugs suffered from heart valve damage. A number of people also died from using the two drugs. The drugs can cause the following side effects:

• Insomnia
• Memory loss
• Depression

Insomnia was just one of the many side effects of taking fen-phen. Many more serious problems occurred from taking the drug.

- Abnormal heart rate
- Damage to nerve endings
- Permanent damage to the heart valves
- Brain damage
- Primary pulmonary hypertension (PPH), a disorder that can be deadly

More Prescription Drugs Replace the Old Ones

The demand for diet drugs continues to be high because many people are willing to take the drugs despite their side effects. Although drug manufacturers have the responsibility to make the medical community and public aware of any potential side effects of the drugs they make and market, doctors need to be vigilant in prescribing the drug in the way it is intended, and patients need to follow their doctors' recommendations and report any side effects immediately. When Redux and fen-phen were taken off the market, people were waiting for something to take their place. They didn't have to wait long.

Meridia

Two months after Redux and fen-phen were recalled, the FDA approved a new drug called sibutramine hydrochloride monohydrate, which was marketed under the name Meridia. It worked by blocking the reuptake of two brain chemicals, serotonin and norepinephrine, which helps users feel full more quickly after eating.

According to Meridia's makers, Abbott Laboratories, the drug was intended for people who need to lose more than 30 pounds (13.6 kilograms). The drugmaker admitted that it could increase blood pressure or heart rate in some patients and should not have been given to patients with uncontrolled or poorly controlled hypertension or a history of heart disease.

In 2002, a consumer watchdog group, Public Citizen, petitioned the FDA to recall Meridia. The group claimed that 397 people had serious adverse reactions to the drug and that it contributed to nineteen deaths, mostly by cardiac arrest. In 2005, the FDA rejected Public Citizen's suggestion to recall the drug. Nonetheless, a number of lawsuits were launched against Abbott Laboratories from people who suffered ill health or whose family members suffered or died after taking Meridia. They claim that Abbott failed to tell users of the serious and potentially fatal side effects. Meridia was eventually withdrawn from the US market in October 2010.

Orlistat

The FDA approved orlistat, marketed under the name Xenical, in 1999. The drug works by blocking some of the fat you eat from being absorbed and digested. This undigested fat is then removed in your bowel movements. Side effects include gas with oily discharge, an increased number of bowel movements, an urgent need to have them, and an inability to control them, particularly after meals containing higher amounts of fat than are recommended. (While taking this pill, each meal should not contain more than 30 percent of calories from fat, according to information reported by the American Society of Health-System Pharmacists, Inc.) Other side effects caused by orlistat include stomach pain and irregular menstrual periods.

The manufacturer of Xenical, Roche Laboratories, recommends the drug for patients who have a body mass index (BMI) of 30 or for those who have a BMI of 27 or greater and other risk factors such as high blood pressure, high cholesterol, heart disease, or diabetes.

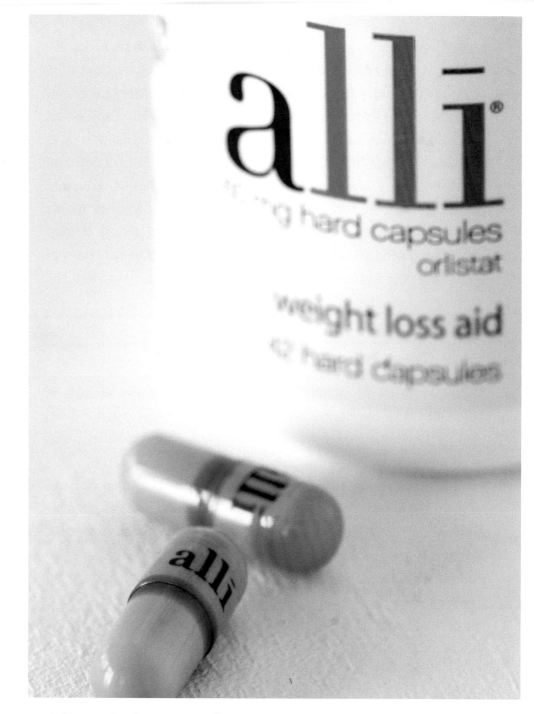

Orlistat, also known as Alli, prevents the body from absorbing fat from food. However, it has many side effects.

Orlistat is now available to consumers in an over-the-counter pill. In early 2006, an FDA advisory committee recommended that drug manufacturer GlaxoSmithKline be able to sell the fat-blocking pill without a doctor's prescription. In 2007, the drug, marketed under the name Alli, was approved for over-the-counter use for weight loss in overweight adults, eighteen years and older, in conjunction with a reduced-calorie and low-fat diet.

These prescription drugs show that weight loss products aren't necessarily safe, even if a doctor says they are. It's important to do your own research and understand that taking any type of medication is a risk.

CHAPTER FOUR

The "Natural" Alternative

Beware of marketing. Companies today are using the word *natural* to market products as healthy. In fact, the word *natural* may not mean natural at all. A lot of times, diet drugs branded as such have just as many unnatural chemicals in them as other products.

Some natural substances can be just as harmful and as strong as prescription drugs. Others need to be used with caution. Some herbal remedies have been used for medicinal purposes in various countries for many years. Taken properly, some may be helpful in relieving certain ailments, but most herbal products have not been subjected to any kind of scientific testing, and there is often no way to determine whether or not they are safe.

Currently, many herbal diet drugs are on the market. Pharmacies may stock some of them, but specialty stores, such as nutrition stores or vitamin stores, are the main suppliers. Today, herbal diet drugs are the best-selling weight-loss products on the US market. Many believe herbal diet drugs are safer than those made from chemicals because herbs are natural.

"Herbal" Fen-Phen

In the late 1990s, the popularity of "herbal fen-phen" skyrocketed: about twelve million Americans used the herbal supplement to suppress appetite and lose weight. The main ingredient in the supplement was ephedra, also known as ma huang. This ingredient,

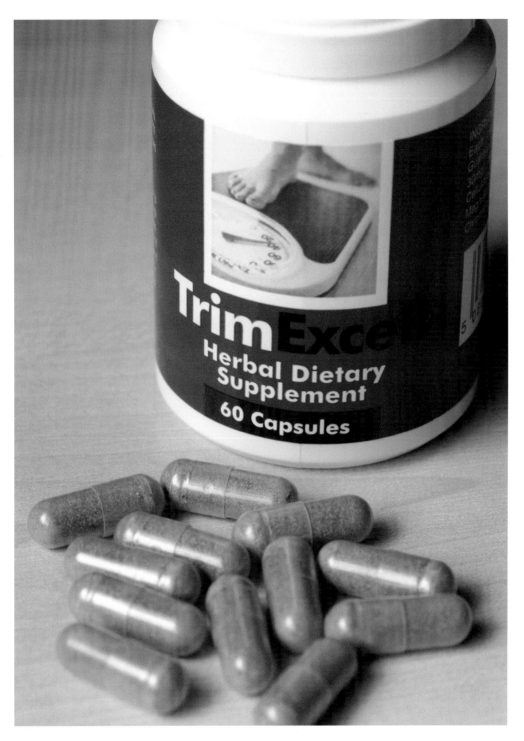

Though herbal dietary supplements may be marketed as all-natural, they aren't necessarily regulated or safe.

used for centuries in China and India to treat asthma and coughs, speeds up the central nervous system, which supposedly can help people burn more calories. But ephedra can also be addictive and have dangerous consequences.

By 2003, ephedra was linked to 155 deaths in the United States. Otherwise healthy people who took over-the-counter products with ephedra suddenly fell ill with heart attacks and stroke. Twenty-three-year-old Baltimore Orioles pitcher Steve Bechler collapsed during spring training of heatstroke and died; the coroner determined that ephedra in his system contributed to his death. Despite protests from manufacturers who made and sold "herbal fen-phen" and other diet supplements containing ephedra, the Food and Drug Administration (FDA) banned all ephedra products from the marketplace.

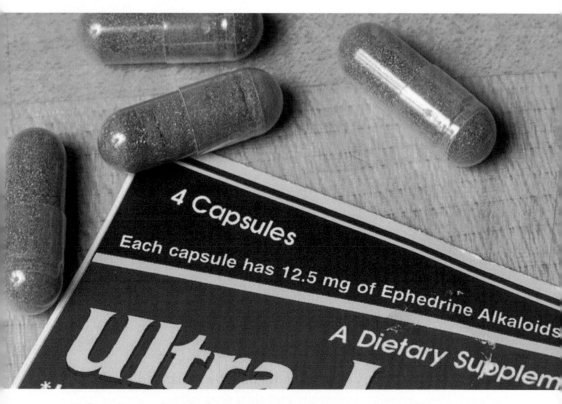

Before it was banned, ephedra was found in many diet supplements.

Non-Ephedra Supplements

After ephedra was banned from the United States, diet supplement manufacturers quickly reformulated their products and released ephedra-free weight-loss remedies.

They typically contain synephrine, otherwise known as bitter orange extract, which is thought to suppress appetite and increase metabolism. Still, researchers have found that the products increase blood pressure and can be particularly dangerous for users who already have hypertension.

Hoodia

People of the San people of southern Africa have long ingested a native succulent (like a cactus) called hoodia, in an effort to ward off hunger and thirst on long treks in the Kalahari Desert. They say it acts like an appetite suppressant. Not surprisingly, the herb *hoodia gordonii* has found its way into weight-loss supplements, from pills and powders to shakes and diet bars—even lollipops. Although the San may have used hoodia for thousands of years, it's a relatively new product introduced to the United States in 2004, so its long-term effectiveness and safety are unknown at this time.

Herbal Dieter's Tea

There are many herbal teas on the market that claim to help people lose weight. But they, too, have serious side effects. The main ingredient in most of these teas is an herb called senna. Senna works as a laxative, and it can cause diarrhea and cramping. If used for a long time, senna depletes the body of potassium, which can cause problems with the heart and colon. Without potassium, the heart beats irregularly. Heart-rhythm disturbances have resulted in many deaths. As a consequence of such deaths, the FDA recommended

Without labels, there's no way to be sure what ingredients are included in a type of diet supplement, such as unpackaged medicinal herbal teas.

that many herbal diet teas carry labels warning that the teas contain laxatives and could cause serious side effects and even death.

In addition to green tea's antioxidants (called catechins) being thought to prevent the growth of cancer, drinking caffeinated green tea has been said to boost metabolism, inhibit fat absorption, and reduce appetite as an aid for weight loss. Green tea is sold as a beverage, in pills, and even as a patch. The FDA has not approved or endorsed green tea as a supplement or treatment for any condition; in fact, people using blood thinners should not drink large amounts of green tea because it could counteract the blood thinners' effectiveness. The moderate health benefits of green tea were well known in Asia long before the drink became popular as a "miracle" weight-loss supplement in the United States.

Energy Pills

Energy pills make no claims of helping a person to lose weight. Instead, they claim to help a person stay with a diet and exercise program. Manufacturers make the assumption that dieting can make a person so weak and tired that he or she won't want to exercise and will be more likely to eat a fattening snack. They claim that energy pills will give you energy. You will then be more likely to stick to your diet and exercise program.

But ask yourself: how do energy pills provide energy? Energy pills contain one or more of the following stimulants: ginseng, green tea, guarana, kola nut, yerba mate, ephedra, and sometimes caffeine. The energy that these substances provide isn't the kind you get from eating healthy foods and exercising regularly. Rather, these substances create a kind of energy that can make you feel anxious and jittery.

FDA Involvement

Another important factor to keep in mind is that the FDA has little control over the sale of herbs. In 1994, the US Congress passed the Dietary Supplement Health and Education Act. This act made it legal to sell so-called natural substances over the counter without FDA testing.

Companies have the right to sell herbs, vitamins, and minerals without testing them to see if they are safe and effective. The only restriction the FDA imposes is to limit the claims that a manufacturer can make for a product. For example, a product cannot claim to cure illness, but it can say how the product affects the body. The end result is a variety of untested products on the market. Without FDA control of the sale of these products, a consumer cannot tell whether they are safe or helpful. Since the FDA doesn't test some of these products, you may be consuming substances that can harm you, maybe not today but down the road.

CHAPTER FIVE

Diet Drugs in Other Forms

Not all diet drugs and weight-loss products come in pill form. There are many new supplements on the market that come as a diet shake or a low-calorie frozen dinner, but these aren't necessarily safe either. These meals are sold in grocery stores and drugstores. The meals are usually available in two forms: as a meal-replacement

Nutrition Facts
Serving Size 1 Can (325 mL)

Amount Per Serving		
Calories (Energy) 190	Fat Cal 50	
		% Daily Value
Total Fat 6g		9%
Saturated Fat 2g		10%
Trans Fat 0g		
Polyunsaturated Fat 1g		
Monounsaturated Fat 3g		
Cholesterol 5mg		2%
Sodium 220mg		9%
Potassium 600mg		17%
Total Carbohydrate 25g		8%
Dietary Fiber 5g		20%
Sugars 18g		20%
Protein 10g		

Vitamin A	35%	•	Vitamin C	15%
Calcium	50%	•	Iron	100%
Vitamin D	35%	•	Vitamin E	35%
Vitamin K	25%	•	Thiamin	35%
Riboflavin	35%	•	Niacin	30%
Vitamin B6	35%	•	Folate	35%
Vitamin B12	35%	•	Biotin	50%
Pantothenic Acid	35%	•	Phosphorus	35%
Iodine	35%	•	Magnesium	35%
Zinc	15%	•	Selenium	35%
Manganese	35%	•	Chromium	35%
Molybdenum	30%			

Percent Daily Values are based on a 2,000 calorie diet.

The New **Slim·Fast!** ③·②·① Plan

pick ② shakes a day

120 Creamy Milk Chocolate

Liquid diet drinks such as those sold under the SlimFast brand have become extremely popular in recent years.

shake or a prepackaged meal. They are generally used to supplement a balanced diet plan, and they should never be eaten as a replacement for a healthy, balanced diet.

These liquid meals and prepackaged diet meals are often expensive. They also may not provide your body with the nutrients it needs. Finally, most people are unable to stick with these low-calorie meals for long. This is because most people need more calories than these meals provide. The body will naturally rebel against a diet that doesn't give the body what it needs. Any weight that is lost often returns after people stop eating the low-calorie meals.

Meals in Liquid Form

One of the problems with liquid meals, otherwise known as meal-replacement shakes, is that they cannot sustain a person for long. It's impossible for one shake to replace an entire meal and still provide the body with the nutrients it needs. Although the package says the liquid diet offers lots of nutrients, the nutrients come from synthetic substances. Synthetic substances cannot give the body the nourishment it needs to develop. This is especially true for teens whose bodies are still growing and developing. The body needs food to fuel its processes.

One brand of liquid meals claims to provide vitamin A, vitamin C, iron, calcium, and many more healthful substances. This sounds good until you read the list of ingredients: sugar, fructose, dextrose, cornstarch, cellulose gel, cupric sulfate, and other chemicals. If you continue reading the label, you learn that skim milk powder is the main source of the vitamins and minerals in the product. (Many meal replacement shakes contain between 200 and 300 calories. You could instead have a large salad full of fresh vegetables and sliced chicken breast, with one tablespoon of light salad dressing, and a small roll for about 250 calories.)

The body needs a certain amount of calories to carry out daily bodily functions. When it doesn't receive the fuel it needs, the results are fatigue and lack of energy. A person may also feel weak or light-headed.

Prepackaged Diet Meals

Two types of prepackaged diet meals are generally available. One kind, such as Weight Watchers, can be purchased at most grocery

Prepackaged diet meals have, in addition to diet drinks, become the convenient supplement of choice for many people. But these, too, have health side effects if abused.

stores. The other kind is available only if you join a weight-loss program, such as Jenny Craig.

Prepackaged diet meals are low in calories, just like the liquid diet shakes. If you purchase them through a weightless program, it can be very expensive. Not only do you have to pay for the costs of the meals, you also need to pay a membership fee to join the program.

People have the same problems with diet meals that they have with diet drinks. It's difficult to stay on a diet that continually deprives the body of the calories and nutrients it needs. Reduced-calorie prepared foods are extremely popular and profitable. The Nestle corporation recently bought the Jenny Craig company for $600 million.

Research indicates that fresh food is healthier and more flavorful than prepackaged food. Some frozen and canned fruits and vegetables can retain more vitamins and nutrients than fresh food because fresh food can lose some nutrients during transit to supermarkets. Preservatives are chemicals that are added to keep many foods from spoiling. Because preservatives are chemicals, they should not be part of every meal.

Follow the Money

One important point that is often overlooked in the discussion of diet pills and weight-loss products is money. The makers of diet pills and weight-loss products are in business to make a profit. In order to do that, they must create a need for their products. The best way to create a need for weight loss products is to convince consumers that being overweight is unhealthy and unattractive.

It's up to you to decide what's attractive…and healthy. Being too thin can be just as unhealthy as being overweight. The important point to remember is to keep everything in balance.

CHAPTER SIX

The Reality of Eating Disorders

Eating disorders are very serious matters that are often about more than food. If you are supplementing your meals with diet drugs, it may be time to take a closer look at what you're trying to achieve.

When a person starts using a weight-loss product in an attempt to lose weight, he or she has started to practice unhealthy weight management. This can lead to a distorted body image and low self-esteem. It can also lead to drug abuse. Abusing any substance, even an over-the-counter product, can be dangerous. Don't make the mistake of thinking that using caffeine, ipecac syrup, or other weight-loss products is a minor matter. If you are abusing diet pills or other weight-loss products, it's important that you speak with someone about your problem. A parent, an older sibling, your doctor, a teacher, or a coach can help you get the help you need.

The Myth of Dieting

The body needs a certain amount of calories every day. The food you eat is converted into fuel for the body to carry on its normal processes. When you don't provide the body with this necessary fuel, it tries to conserve fuel to survive by slowing down its metabolism, or the rate at which the body burns calories. When this metabolic rate is lowered, the body burns fewer calories and stores fat more efficiently.

One of the symptoms of eating disorders is a distorted sense of one's own body weight.

When you eat fewer calories than your body needs, your body may respond by holding on to any food it gets. When a person goes off the diet, the body will regain all the weight lost during the diet, if not more. This is because the metabolism does not return to normal after a diet.

In addition to being ineffective, dieting can also physically damage the body. The teen years are a time of great mental and physical growth. During this period, your body is changing from a child's body into an adult's. Your body needs fuel to make this transformation successfully. If it fails to receive this fuel, important bodily functions, such as a young woman's menstruation, may be delayed. A lack of nutrients can also lead to osteoporosis, a disease that weakens the bones.

Another danger of dieting is the attitude it can create. When a diet is unsuccessful, a person's self-esteem suffers. You may feel like a failure when weight is not lost permanently. You can begin an unhealthy cycle of yo-yo dieting. Yo-yo dieting is when a person begins and quits a diet several times. You may begin to lose touch with reality and become desperate in the quest to lose weight. Taking diet pills or other weight-loss products is only the beginning of an unhealthy pattern of behavior. It is possible that this pattern may eventually lead to the development of an eating disorder.

When Dieting Becomes an Eating Disorder

Eating disorders include anorexia nervosa, bulimia nervosa, and binge eating disorder (compulsive eating). Compulsive exercise (also called exercise addiction) is also a growing problem and is classified by experts as an eating disorder–related problem. A

Anorexia nervosa is a serious eating disorder that must be treated immediately by a qualified professional.

person can have one or more of these disorders, and anyone can suffer from them—men and women of all ages and backgrounds.

According to the Eating Disorder Foundation, victims of eating disorders generally have very low self-esteem. The National Eating Disorders Association reported that five million to ten million females and one million males in the United States have an eating disorder such as anorexia nervosa and bulimia nervosa.

While most eating disorders affect females, an increasing number of males are developing them. About one out of every ten people with an eating disorder is male, according to the National Association of Anorexia Nervosa and Associated Disorders, Inc. An eating disorder is extremely dangerous physically and mentally. If it is not treated properly, it can lead to permanent damage and even death.

Anorexia

People with anorexia nervosa intentionally starve themselves to lose weight. People with anorexia have a weight that is at least 15 percent below what is considered normal. High self-esteem and a healthy body image help young women avoid the negative thoughts and emotions that lead to an eating disorder. The problem is that no matter how much weight is lost, people with anorexia never think it is enough. Anorexia causes people to see their bodies in a distorted manner. People with anorexia believe they are too fat and need to lose more weight.

Bulimia

People with bulimia nervosa often engage in unhealthy bingeing and purging cycles. People with bulimia nervosa binge, or eat a lot of food in one sitting, often eating without control. They then try to purge the food from their bodies by various methods. These methods include inducing vomiting, taking laxatives or other products (such as diuretics), or exercising for long periods of time.

Compulsive Behaviors

People who compulsively exercise also have a distorted body image. They believe they are fat and will exercise for hours at a time every day, often secretly, so they will continue to lose weight. They may also force themselves to vomit or abuse diet pills and/or laxatives.

Compulsive exercising, or exercising too much to lose weight, can also be a type of disorder. Once the symptoms appear, it is important to seek professional help.

People who eat compulsively often use food as a way to cope with problems in their lives. They have an unhealthy relationship with food, and they need help to deal with their problems. Unlike other eating disorders, people suffering from compulsive eating are not trying to lose weight. These people may eat large amounts of food, but they will not try to rid the body of the food.

It's important to note that the symptoms of these eating disorders are interchangeable. This means a person with bulimia may also try to starve himself or herself, and a person with anorexia may also exercise compulsively. It is also important to remember that there is no single cause for an eating disorder and no single cure. Eating disorders can be linked to feelings of low self-esteem, emotional problems, family problems, abuse (including sexual abuse), and even life changes and transitions.

Know the Warning Signs

Some common signs of an eating disorder include the following:

- Constantly thinking about the size and shape of your body
- Constantly thinking about how much you weigh and weighing yourself repeatedly during the day
- Constantly thinking about food, cooking, and eating
- Eating only certain foods in specific and limited amounts
- Keeping a list of what foods are OK to eat
- Wanting to eat alone and feeling uncomfortable eating with other people
- Not feeling good about yourself unless you are thin, but never being satisfied with how thin you are
- Thinking that you should exercise more, no matter how much you do exercise

- Feeling competitive about dieting and wanting to be the thinnest or the smallest
- Taking diet pills or laxatives
- Continuing to diet, even after you are thin
- Purposely losing lots of weight very quickly
- Forcing yourself to throw up
- No longer having your monthly period

If anything on this list describes you, you may have an eating disorder. You don't have to have every symptom on the list to have an eating disorder. If some of these sound familiar, consider getting help.

Understand the Dangers

Much like any addiction, eating disorders are difficult to stop and are destructive to your health. According to the Renfrew Center in Philadelphia, Pennsylvania, an eating disorder treatment facility, eating disorders have the highest mortality rate of any mental illness—almost 20 percent.

Even with professional help, it is an ongoing process to recover from an eating disorder, but many people do recover and live successful, healthy lives. If you think you may be suffering from one or more of these eating disorders, it's important that you reach out for help. Talk to someone you trust and seek professional help. You can contact organizations such as Anorexia Nervosa and Related Eating Disorders, Inc., the National Association of Anorexia Nervosa and Associated Disorders, or the National Eating Disorders Association, among others, for more information and resources in your area. With the proper help, you can begin to recover from the disorder and take back control of your life.

CHAPTER SEVEN

Healthy Mind, Healthy Body

Popular culture often tells people to be unhappy with their bodies. Every magazine stand, gossip website, and television program equates thinness with beauty. It tells people they need to achieve an ideal body shape that is impossible for most. The best thing you can do for yourself right now is to learn to accept your body and try to lead a healthy lifestyle.

During your teen years, when your body is growing and developing, it's important to provide your body with the proper nutrients. But if you put yourself on a restrictive diet and replace meals with diet pills and other weight-loss products, you are depriving your body of the nutrients it needs to grow and develop properly. Not only does dieting hurt your body, but it is also ineffective. It can lead to other serious conditions, such as an eating disorder or addiction to substances that you believe help you lose weight.

Your weight is merely one indicator of your overall health. Unfortunately, many dieters focus narrowly on achieving a "perfect" weight. Ask yourself why you want to lose weight. Do you think you will be happier or healthier if you lose weight? If you do, it's important to recognize that many leading health experts now question the importance of weight. Being healthy involves much more than a number on a scale. Being healthy means eating well and exercising regularly. It's also important to remember that your worth as a person is not connected with your weight.

There's no problem with wanting to be fit as long as it's done in a healthy manner, such as through regular exercise and a sensible diet.

Accept Yourself

Each person is born with genes that determine how he or she will look physically, from the color of the eyes, to height, to the type of body he or she will have. These are qualities that make each of us unique. No matter how hard some people may try or what kind of diet they go on, they will never look like a supermodel. According to the National Eating Disorders Association, the average American female is 5 feet 4 inches (1.6 meters) tall and weighs 140 pounds (63.5 kilograms), whereas the average American fashion model is 5 feet 11 inches (1.8 m) in height and weighs 117 pounds (53 kg).

Many teens often fall into the trap of comparing themselves to the beautiful, thin people in movies, on television, and in advertisements. Some teens believe the people they see in the media are the norm. But if you take a look around at the people in your life—your friends, family, classmates, and even the people you see on the street—you'll realize that there are many different body types and many different kinds of beauty. You'll also notice that not many people look like the people in the movies or ads.

No one is perfect. This includes the people you see in the media. We all have qualities that make each of us unique and special. This is why you should never compare yourself to another person. You have unique qualities that no one else has. Learn to accept yourself—emotionally and physically.

Improve Your Self-Confidence

One of the best ways to avoid comparing yourself to others is to build your self-confidence. Have faith in your abilities and yourself. When you feel good about and believe in yourself, you are less likely to be tempted to try to change yourself. Confidence is the

Magazines often give young people a distorted view of what society sees as beauty.

foundation of good mental and physical health. The next time you start putting yourself down, stop and tell yourself:

- I will remember that being thin does not make me a happier person.
- I will stop comparing my body with other people's bodies.
- I will exercise because it's fun and healthy, not because it burns calories.
- I will do things that make me feel good about myself and that don't revolve around my body shape and size.
- I will value other people for who they are, not what they look like.

One of the best defenses against negative body image is self-confidence. Learn to love who you are, and a positive body image will follow.

Exercise and Eat Right

Eating nutritious foods and exercising regularly will go a long way to improve the quality of your life. While you now know that dieting is unhealthy, it does not mean that you shouldn't think about what you eat.

Eating well-balanced meals of lean meats, fruits, nuts, vegetables, milk and other dairy products, and whole grains is an important part of healthy eating. While it's important to avoid too much sugar, salt, or caffeine, healthy eating does not mean that you have to completely deprive yourself.

Eating right involves having a variety of foods, including those from all the major food groups.

Everyone has a busy life, and each person cannot eat sensibly all the time. There will also be times when you crave a candy bar or French fries, and it's perfectly fine to give in to the craving occasionally.

The secret is moderation. Keep your meals balanced. Always make your health a priority, not a number on a scale or the size of your clothes. When you don't routinely deny yourself the foods you want, you are more likely to eat well overall.

Exercise is also an important part of staying fit and healthy. It is recommended that a person exercise for thirty minutes or more daily. This does not mean that you have to go to the gym every day and work out for hours at a time. You should make exercising into a fun activity. Go biking with a friend, try Rollerblading, or go for a long walk. Join the school track team. Do anything that you enjoy and that gets you on your feet and your heart beating faster.

You should not think of exercise just as a way to lose weight. If you do, you may become frustrated when you fail to see the results you want. There are many benefits to exercise. It helps to strengthen your body. It increases your confidence in yourself and your body. It reduces stress and makes you feel good.

Speak Out Against Diet Culture

Even after you learn everything about the dangers of diet drugs, it's not easy to give up the idea of dieting and accept yourself at whatever size you happen to be. Every day, you may encounter images and messages from family, friends, and society that praise the thin and punish the fat. These ideas are hard to ignore. But you are not powerless against them. Speaking out against fat prejudice and diet culture is a great way to improve your own self-esteem and create awareness about the dangers of diets.

Create a support group at your school or among your friends. Write a letter to a television network or fashion magazine when you see images that you don't like. Talk to your parents and teachers about what you've learned about the dangers of diet drugs. All these things will help you develop a healthy self-image that will give you the confidence to keep a positive attitude about food and weight for the rest of your life.

When it comes to weight, it's important for you to stand up and be a leader. Show your peers that beauty is not about how much or little you weigh. It's about having confidence in yourself and your body image.

10 GREAT QUESTIONS TO ASK YOUR DOCTOR

1. Is there such a thing as a healthy diet drug?

2. I tried losing weight naturally but it hasn't worked. Should I turn to diet drugs?

3. When do I know if I have an eating disorder?

4. What's a realistic weight-loss goal I should set for myself?

5. I see celebrities endorsing diet drugs all the time. Does this mean they're safe?

6. What should I do if I think I have an eating disorder?

7. What is a healthy way to lose weight?

8. What is a healthy weight for my height and body type?

9. When do I know if I'm abusing my diet drugs?

10. What if I can't lose weight by any means?

ANOREXIA NERVOSA An eating disorder in which a person refuses to eat and keeps losing weight.

APPETITE SUPPRESSANT A drug that is supposed to control hunger.

BINGE EATING DISORDER (COMPULSIVE EATING) An eating disorder in which a person eats large amounts of food but does not purge.

BODY MASS INDEX A popular method used to gauge whether or not a person is overweight. BMI is calculated by dividing a person's weight (in kilograms) by his or her height (in meters, squared).

BULIMIA NERVOSA An eating disorder in which a person eats large amounts of food and then gets rid of it by purging.

CALORIE In scientific terms, a calorie is the energy require to raise the temperature of one gram of water one degree Celsius.

DIURETIC (WATER PILL) A drug that causes an increase in the amount of urine put out by the kidneys.

EATING DISORDER Any of a range of abnormal eating habits (such as anorexia nervosa).

FALSE ADVERTISING Misrepresentation of a product, which may negatively affect consumers.

FOOD AND DRUG ADMINISTRATION (FDA) The US government agency responsible for protecting the public health by regulating food and drug products.

HERBAL Any product made from herbs, especially those used in cooking and medicine.

LAXATIVE A substance that causes bowel movements.

NUTRIENT Any substance that provides nourishment.

PRESCRIPTION A note from a doctor that allows a person to purchase a regulated drug.

PRESERVATIVE A chemical used to preserve foods.

PURGE To rid the body of food or calories.

SEROTONIN A chemical substance in the brain that regulates mood and appetite.

SIDE EFFECT Undesirable secondary effect of a drug.

STIMULANT An herb, drug, or other substance that activates the nervous system.

American Diabetes Association
1701 North Beauregard Street
Alexandria, VA 22311
(800) 342-2383
Website: http://www.diabetes.org
The American Diabetes Association fights and advocates for
those affected by diabetes by funding research to prevent,
cure, and manage diabetes.

American Dietetic Association
Headquarters
Academy of Nutrition and Dietetics
120 South Riverside Plaza, Suite 2000
Chicago, IL 60606-6995
(800) 877-1600
Website: http://www.eatright.org
This organization offers information on food and nutrition for
maintaining a healthy diet and can refer you to a registered
dietitian or nutritionist in your area.

American Heart Association
7272 Greenville Avenue
Dallas, TX 75231
Website: http://www.heart.org
1-800-AHA-USA-1
The American Heart Association is the nation's oldest and
largest voluntary organization dedicated to fighting heart
disease and stroke. It also offers recommendations for
maintaining a healthy diet and lifestyle.

National Association of Anorexia Nervosa and Associated
    Disorders (ANAD)
750 E Diehl Road #127
Naperville, IL 60563
(630) 577-1330
Website: http://www.anad.org
ANAD is the country's oldest nonprofit organization dedicated
    to alleviating the problems of eating disorders and promot-
    ing healthy lifestyles.

National Eating Disorders Association
165 West 46th Street
Suite 402
New York, NY 10036
Administrative Office: (212) 575-6200
Website: http://www.nationaleatingdisorders.org
NEDA is a nonprofit organization dedicated to educating the
    public about the prevention of eating disorders. It promotes
    access to quality treatment for those affected by eating
    disorders and helps support their families through educa-
    tion, advocacy, and research.

Overeaters Anonymous (OA)
PO Box 44020
Rio Rancho, NM 8717 4-4020
(SOS) 891-2664
Website: http://www.overeatersanonymous.org
OA is a fellowship of individuals who are recovering from com-
    pulsive overeating. OA meetings are held at thousands of
    locations throughout the country and world. The meetings
    offer support and encouragement for individuals of all ages;

meeting structure follows the twelve-step program made popular by Alcoholics Anonymous. Visit the Web site to find a meeting near you.

Websites

Because of the changing nature of Internet links, Rosen Publishing has developed an online list of websites related to the subject of this book. This site is updated regularly. Please use this link to access the list:

http://www.rosenlinks.com/CED/Diet

FOR FURTHER READING

American Heart Association. *No-fad Diet: A Personal Plan for Healthy Weight Loss*. New York, NY: Clarkson Potter Publishers, 2011.

Bijlefeld, Marjolijn. *Encyclopedia of Diet Fads: Understanding Science and Society*. Santa Barbara, CA: Greenwood Group, 2014.

Costin, Carolyn, and Gwen Schubert Grabb. *8 Keys to Recovery from an Eating Disorder: Effective Strategies from Therapeutic Practice and Personal Experience*. New York, NY: W. W. Norton, 2012.

Fairburn, Christopher G. *Overcoming Binge Eating: The Proven Program to Learn Why You Binge and How You Can Stop*. New York, NY: The Guilford Press, 2013.

Fitzgerald, Matt. *Diet Cults: The Surprising Fallacy at the Core of Nutrition Fads and a Guide to Healthy Eating ... for the Rest of Us*. New York, NY: Pegasus, 2015.

Hansen, Kathryn. *Brain over Binge: Why I Was Bulimic, Why Conventional Therapy Didn't Work, and How I Recovered for Good*. Phoenix, AZ: Camellia Pub., 2011.

Hornbacher, Marya. *Wasted: A Memoir of Anorexia and Bulimia*. New York, NY: HarperCollins, 2014.

Jaminet, Paul, and Shou-Ching Jaminet. *Perfect Health Diet: Regain Health and Lose Weight by Eating the Way You Were*

Meant to Eat. New York, NY: Scribner, 2012.

Poppink, Joanna. *Healing Your Hungry Heart: Recovering from Your Eating Disorder*. San Francisco, CA: Conari/RedWheel/Weiser, 2011.

Rockridge Press. *The Clean Eating Cookbook & Diet: Over 100 Healthy Whole Food Recipes & Meal Plans*. Berkeley, CA: Rockridge, 2013.

About the Authors

Nicholas Faulkner is a writer living in New Jersey. Kara Williams is a writer living in New York.

Photo Credits